# Diary of A MisEducated Baby Mama

Tamykah Anthony-Marston

# DEDICATION

To the Baby Mama whose Mama never taught her how to
be a Mama.
To the Baby Mama who loved too hard.
To the Baby Mama who gave up on her dreams to provide
for her children.
To the Baby Mama who gets no help.
To the Baby Mama trying to co-parent with a non-parent.
To the Baby Mama who cries daily.
To the Baby Mama who thinks no man will love her
because she has children.
To the Baby Mama who feels inadequate.


To the Father raising children not his own.
To the Baby Daddy who makes empty promises.
To the Father who repairs broken hearts.
To the Baby Daddy who didn't have a Daddy.
To the Baby Daddy who is ready to be a Father.

# CONTENTS

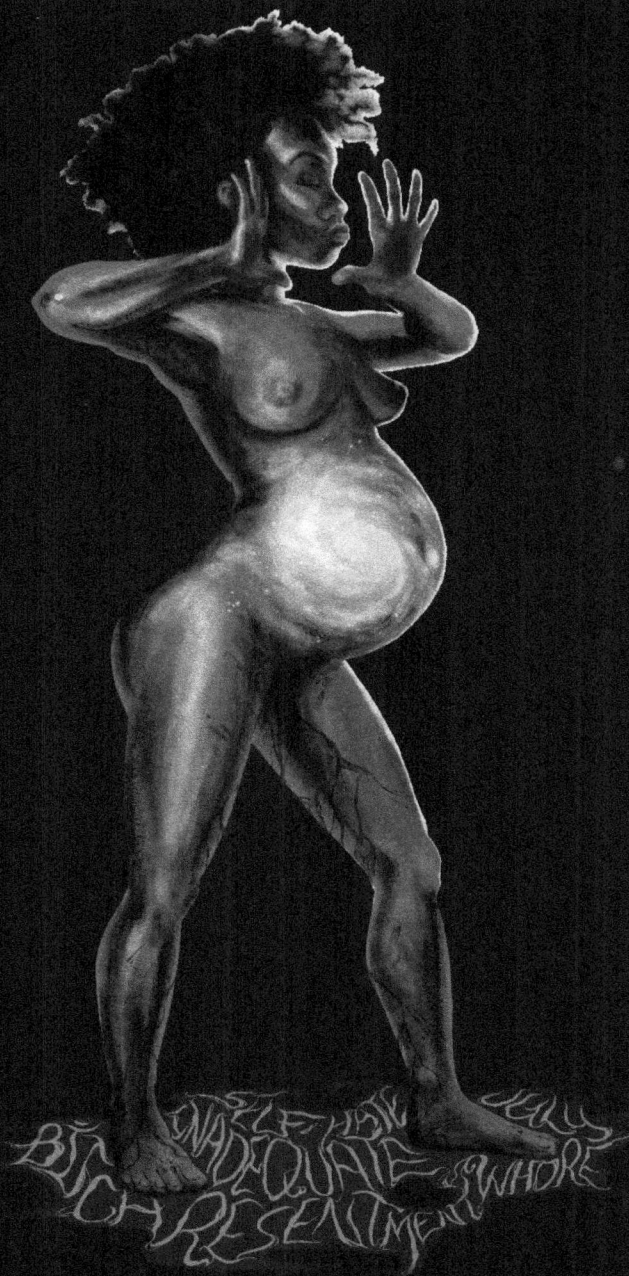

# ACKNOWLEDGMENTS

To my three heartbeats Nevaeh, Sameer and Usha. Thank you for choosing me

To my Loving husband Lashawn "Suga Ray" Marston. Thank you for softening my heart.

# FIRST
# TRIMESTER

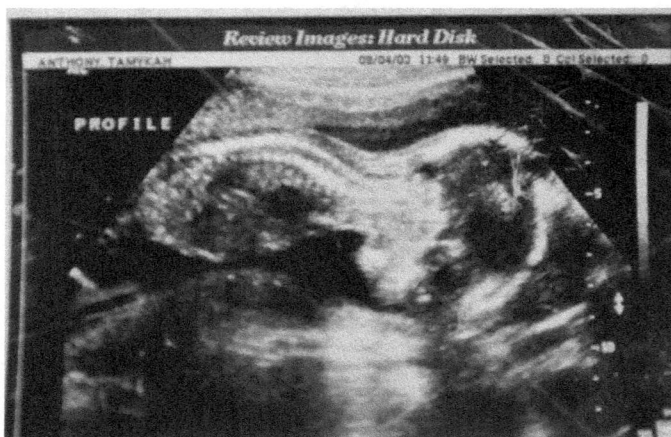

Overwhelming, unexpected, unseen changes. It was something no one could have prepared me for. In the blink of an eye, everything was different. The transformation into a parent. I was experiencing things I had never experienced before. The pain, the disappointment and the struggle that severely bruised and almost broke me. Emotionally. Mentally. Physically. I was growing through so much but no one could see it. I didn't know it then and it would be years before I finally understood but it was my first real lesson in Faith....I could not see the transformation happening inside me but the universe was developing me like an embryo....teaching me....helping me lay the foundation and formulate the blueprint that would teach me how to forever transform my pain into purpose. I was hurting. My body was aching and my heart was torn, yet my soul was filled with joy. Life was happening. I was grateful, but still afraid. I was excited, but still apprehensive. I was ready to usher life into this world, but yet I wasn't even sure I wanted to live.

# **Reflections**

I thought I hated myself
but I couldn't kill myself
so there was still a piece of me that I loved deep
down
I searched for this piece in the mirror but It was not
there
I let others penetrate me so they could help me find It
but they seemed to push It deeper down with their
angry appendages
because every time they were done,
It felt farther away....
then I found It....
in my womb.

You are me, so loving you I learned how to love me.
Loving myself through my reflection in your pretty
brown eyes Baby Girl.

# **Teenage Mother**

I was always smart...so they said...and I believed them
But how could a smart girl make such a stupid
mistake...so they said
You ruined your life...so they said
Everything you would've been is gone...so they said
You will never be anything now...so they said
Their belief in me is the only reason I believed in
myself so they had to be right this time too...Right?
I accepted all of their truths as my own for a long
time. It was easy to not have to try.
Then one day I looked into HER eyes and I couldn't
let them tell her what they told me....I couldn't let
them make her believe it...I looked at the path behind
me and I couldn't let her follow in those footsteps.
GAMECHANGER
This smart girl remembered her passions
This smart girl went to college
This smart girl made the Dean's List every semester
This smart girl even made another stupid mistake and
got knocked up again a year before graduation
But this smart...stupid teenage mother became a
Scientist.
What do you think THEY are saying now?

TAMYKAH ANTHONY-MARSTON

# Contractions

Contractions are like roller coaster rides.
As you're going up watching the scenery
around...ascending....

Everything looks wonderful...promising....
Then you get to the top and realize the journey
ahead....
the plummet...the fluctuations...the changes

And the fear sets in...fear and pain
You want to go back but the only way out is down.....
28 hours and 200 contractions later....you unbuckle
your seatbelt and enter a whole new ride.

# Love at First Breath, Fear at First Cry

While I nurtured you within me, I saw you in my dreams many times before I laid eyes on you.

In each dream you looked different...a different combination of genotypes and phenotypes.

In each dream, I practiced feeding you, rocking you, clothing you...my idea of what motherhood was.

I fell in Love when I heard that unfamiliar rhythm of your heartbeat.

I had already danced with the idea that it would just be the two of us on this journey and I was prepared...so I thought.

You had a rocky entry into the world ... Car accident, fetal distress, induction, contractions, long labor.........
Then I heard you cry...the scariest moment in my life thus far.

# Curse of a Single Mother

Watching your child hurt from the words or actions
of someone else is a rage like no other

Empty promises from a baby daddy to his
daughter...days of watching baby girl sit on the
radiator in the living room waiting on Daddy...scared
to move for fear that he may pass by, look up at the
window and not see her there and leave...empty
graduation seats saved for Daddy...molded pieces of
birthday cake saved for Daddy...days of listening to
and watching phone conversations ending in week
long tears over Daddy....

You keep doing what you can as a mother but it is
never enough...all she wants is Daddy.

As the years pass, a change happens....
Baby Girl goes from asking "Mommy what's wrong
with me....why doesn't he love me?" to Big Girl
spewing "It's your fault Mommy!"

As much as it hurts, you take the hurt for her...you let
her words slice deep into your already overworked
soul so she won't have to deal with the reality...
"He doesn't want to be a father, Baby Girl"

8

# Call Me Daddy

"Ooh, Call me Daddy"

Why does a stranger calling you Daddy arouse your penis

Yet when your heartbroken daughter cries for Daddy it doesn't stimulate your soul?

# The Birds and the Bees

A father is a girl's First love....

Her first standard of a man's love
Her first standard of how a man should treat her
Her first standard of how a man should make her feel
This relationship is the blueprint.

If he is never around, she will search for him in the
arms of hungry boys and men.

If he doesn't tell her she is beautiful, she will fall in
love with the first predator who tells her she's cute.

If he doesn't teach her about those sneaky boys, she
will mistake lust for love.

If he doesn't give her affection, she will allow men to
ravage her body just to be touched.

If he doesn't treat her like a princess, she will never
expect to be treated like a Queen.

A father is a girl's First Love
The first and last man she should ever call Daddy.

# Child Support

50 dollars can buy a pair of sneakers
But not the memory of you teaching her how to tie
her shoe.

100 dollars can buy a graduation outfit
But not the sweet sound of your voice in the audience
cheering her name.

80 dollars can buy a new bike
But not the memory of you putting Band-Aids on her
bruises after a fall.

10 dollars can buy medicine
But not the hours in the ER comforting her.

40 dollars can pay for a new hairstyle
But not her bubbly smile after Daddy tells her she's
beautiful.

Child "support".....smh

# WHAT IF?

What would happen if you cared for your daughter
who took 9 months to perfect

The same way you cared for those Jordans Nike took
9 seconds to throw together?

# FORGIVENESS

Do I need to forgive you for not being in her life...for making her cry....

Or

Do I need to forgive myself for choosing you to procreate with?

# PUSSY

I would never call you a pussy to symbolize weakness
or insult you

In fact me calling you a pussy is an insult to pussies
everywhere.

Pussy bleeds every month and doesn't die

Pussy brings great men to their knees...Literally!

Pussy can turn the hardest man soft

Pussy stretches like a watermelon through the eye of a
needle and then snaps right back

Pussy pushes out Kings and Queens

There is no procreation without pussy

Pussy is the center of the universe

Pussy is powerful

You could never be a pussy on your best day!

# MISOGYNY

When do we stop telling our young queens that when
a boy hits her, that means he likes her?

At what point did physical violence become a reason
to be flattered?

I'm not sure if I was told this as a child, but I do
remember hearing it somewhere.

It did not hit me until HE hit me that this was a lie!

Eye quickly swelling and throbbing from the punch in
the face,

I did not feel LOVED or even LIKED in that
moment

I felt hated

As I fell to the floor, I looked up to see my baby girl
wide eyed and scared at what she saw

She didn't see Love or Like either!
She saw hate
She felt fear

And that is a moment she has always remembered.
Her first lesson that
Violence, pain and hurt are no part of the LOVE
equation

# SECOND TRIMESTER

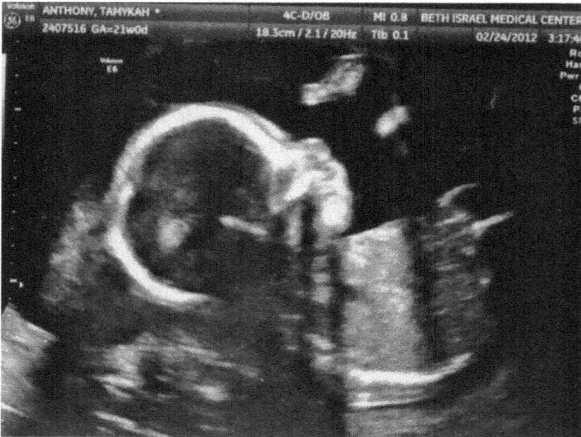

Ahh yes, I can finally breathe! Life is starting to make sense. It was all for a reason; the sleepless nights, the tear-filled days, the pain, the agony, the discomfort. It would all get easier from here. I felt so connected to it all. I understood. I thought I had finally gotten it right, but I was searching for something in him that I should've found in myself....and he was ready and willing to feed me the lies that I hungrily digested in my broken womb. Suddenly, the air became thin. I was suffocating. In that moment, I was reminded that New Life wasn't birthed just yet...and this time, this trimester, I learned, may have been more painful than the first. I realized that there was still a little time left before the pain would completely cease

# **Unintentional Side Chick**

You told me you loved me... I believed you

You told me we would be a family... I believed you.

I needed to believe you

Excitement about the life growing within and being
able to share that with someone...Finally!

December 2011...3 months pregnant and glowing
from the thoughts of happiness and being in love
with the idea of being loved
No more baby mama title
I messed up once already
It's finally happening

December 2011...phone rings waking me up from
beautiful dreams of shared milestones.
All your lies brought to the surface
All the lies I told myself now floating away and
becoming more distant as I hear each word.

What...wait...this can't be happening...world
shattered....
I touch my growing belly, fingers tracing apologies to
my son
Months later my King is born....5 weeks later his
brother is born.

You do the math

Status upgraded from baby mama to baby mama
AND unintentional side chick

Welcome to the world baby boy

# Letter to my Queens

Dear Queens,

These confused and misguided men who disrespect us after we have grown, carried and birthed their seed are scared.

It's Fear.

It's the same reason white people try to kill us and destroy us....they are scared of us.

Once that *nigga* sees you take his seed into the micro universe that is your womb and transform life from a pencil dot to an 8 pound being, creating organs and tissues and nerves inside you.
Once he sees you experiencing pain kin to multiple bones being broken at the same time...and then not die and emerge stronger....

He is filled with fear and maybe even a little envy.

He realizes he has just met a GOD.

# The Facade

It took some time

But I see now that I was never in love with you.

I was in love with the idea of you loving me in spite of me not loving myself

Every time you entered me I derived pleasure NOT from your stiff appendage and lust filled tongue massages....
No, I derived pleasure from the fact that, in that moment, I was good enough to give you such unthinkable pleasure...to make you feel good....make you feel better than I could make myself feel.

# Confused Soul

How do you get wet for a man who does not take
care of the children he has with other women?

Oh yea I forgot...cuz you're different and he really
loves you because you got that *good good*

I have been there done that...and might I add
probably better than you...please don't make my
mistakes.

Don't confuse your convenience with your worth to
him.

# Carnal Exchange

Once you stop giving up pieces of your dignity
through the warmth and wetness of your vagina,
Visits stop
Financial help stops
Single parenthood officially begins.

Once you find that MAN that loves every inch of you
including your extensions (your babies),
Resentment sets in
Insults start
Disrespect ensues.

So this is the tradeoff...as long as you keep giving up
access to your juices, he remains in his child's life.
Do you sell your soul to buy time for your child with
his father?

Deal with the Devil

# **Tha Struggle**

24 hours in a day
Work for 10 hours
Sleep for 6 hours (on a good day)
Doing homework with them for 2 hours
Making doctors' appointments for 1 hour
Attend classes to complete your degree for 3 hours
Study for your classes for 2 hours
Cooking meals for 2 hours
Cleaning for 30 minutes
Spending time with them for 2 hours
Making sure they eat breakfast, brush their teeth and
get dressed for 45 minutes
Taking a shower and getting yourself dressed 10
minutes
Shuffling and postdating bills for 30 min
Crying and praying for 10 minutes
Taking a breath for 10 seconds

Who says we have no superpowers....we bend time
and space every day!

# MISOGYNY PART II

When you called me a bitch

When you pushed me down

When you ripped "our" son from my arms while my
daughter and your other son watched

When my daughter, so scared, had to call 911

When you left me bleeding on the floor while your
son cried for milk and I couldn't get to him

You never loved me

But yet my body and spirit were so powerful that I
was able to transform your hateful and tormented
seed and allow the spiteful parts of you to combust
inside me and never reach the life we created.

# Mother to Son

Your love makes up for what I missed from my
Father
Your hugs soothe my heart that ached from your
Father
You are Great
You are Amazing
I will spend every breath reminding you of the King
you are.
You are my Hopes and Dreams for the Black Man.

# Daughters

Would you be okay with your daughter being treated
the same way he treats you?!
No....
Aren't you someone's daughter too?

Would you be okay with another man treating your
daughter the same way you treat her?!
No....
Isn't she someone's daughter too?

# Regret

Laying on my side staring out the window into the
alternate universe I thought would be my life.
Head on pillow.... hand cupped in between.
The tears run from one eye, over the bridge of my
nose and into the other eye before finally sliding
down my face onto the waiting pillow

# Black Man

He has cursed me
Beat me
Trampled my name and used my body
But yet I love the Black Man

He has left me to raise a daughter alone
Left me to teach a son how to be a man
Left me with regret and heartache
But yet I love the Black King

He has called me Ugly
Told me I was too black
Ridiculed my stretch marks
But yet I love the Black God

He has called me a Bitch with the same mouth that
suckled at my nipple for comfort because his Mama
never gave it to him
The same Bitch's nipple that nourished his son...the
extension of his seed and legacy
But yet I love the Black Emperor
There is nothing more transformative than the LOVE
of a Black Queen.
We carry our men on our shoulders even as they
suffocate us with their embedded hate...
We have suffered and died for His sins
Jesus aint got nuthin on us

# Questions without Answers

Why plant a seed if you have no intention of being
PRESENT
To nurture it, protect it, water it and watch its
growth?

# DIARY OF A MISEDUCTED BABY MAMA

# THIRD
# TRIMESTER

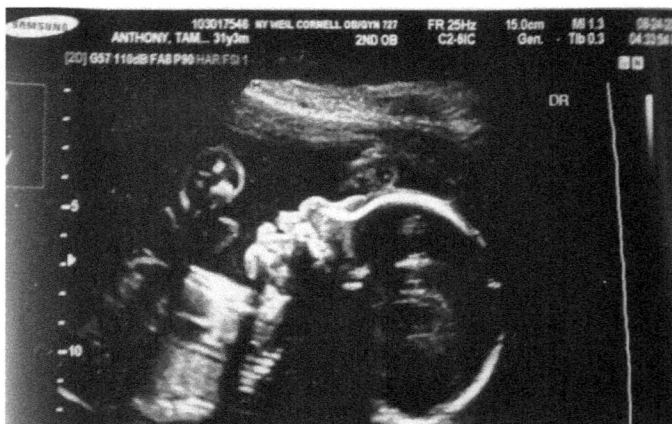

All the ground work is over and it is now time for monumental and explosive growth. The end of the pain and discomfort is nearer but not before the excruciating climax. It is going to get way worse before it gets better. As I watch my growth, I realize how each of the previous trimesters led up to this.....had I not gone through all that I did, this would not have been appreciated or even possible! As my body was being reorganized to carry new life, my heart was being transformed and healed for new beginnings.

All the sacrifices were worth it!

# **Love**

When you find that King whose love inspires you to
love yourself unconditionally.

When you become the Queen whose reflection you
see when you look in his eyes.

When he is willing to cut his fingers putting the sharp
broken pieces of you back together.

When you allow your heart, body, soul and womb to
open again.

# Call me Crazy

How did we meet and get married 4 months later?

They called me crazy...some called me delusional

But let me ask you this

What about those who are in long relationships waiting for their partners to become spouse material?

Is that not crazy?

Is that not delusional?

There was no wait needed....

What others wait years to see,
I saw in days

What others wait years to feel,
I felt in weeks

What others wait years to Know,
I Knew in months.
Call me Crazy!

# **Your Eyes**

I see the way you look at me

Through me

In me

Finding beauty in every move I make, every word I
say, every breath I take

It terrifies me!

# **Baby Mama to Wife**

How do you go from solo to team?
From alone to partner?
From jaded to joyful?
From resentful to loving?
From anger to understanding?
From single to married?

Not without a fight!

I fought for my old life....
Still do sometimes
Even though I wasn't happy
I got comfortable in the self-loathe
I got comfortable with the disappointment
I got comfortable talking about my struggles
I wore my single mother badge as my greatest feat of
strength.

Even though I had always wanted a true partner, I
fought to keep my "Baby Mama" title because it was
so embedded in my identity and I didn't know how to
be anything else.

# Stretchmarks

Light against dark skin
Red against light skin.

Intricate pathways intertwining and branching like the
tree of life.

Textured to the touch...beautiful like the stripes on
the Tiger.

Complex system of lines signifying the blood vessels
and neurons sprouting in the life within you.
You literally carry the future.

Each new life form adding its own storylines to the
masterpiece your body was chosen to display.

As special and unique as a fingerprint
Celebrate your Life Prints, Queens.

# Special Breed

To those men who love and care for children who do
not carry their DNA,

You are appreciated.

To those men who wipe the tears of the child whose
father never shows up and hold the hands of the
mothers struggling to do it alone.

You are amazing.
You are Fathers.

# **Untitled**

She grew and thrived inside me as I watched the news
wondering what protection I could really give her
outside my womb.

How do I carry this Queen while watching them
murder fathers and uncles and grandfathers of
potential husbands who will never get to experience
her Love or her Beauty?

# Dawn: Daughter of Heaven

The Dr said "you sure picked a bad time to get pregnant"

But I knew she was wrong.

My eyes filled with blood, growths on my brain, blindness, syncope...dangerous falls.

But you held on and gave me another reason to hold on.

The Dr said " this baby could kill you or heal you"

I only entertained the latter.

You healed my body, my heart, my soul.

The bigger you grew inside me, the smaller the doubt that I could do all things.

You woke up the sleeping God inside me.

# **Labels**

3 children...3 baby daddies

Is she a ho?

Is she loose?

Is she uneducated?

Is she a hoodrat?

Is she not wife-material?

Is she a bad mother?

Is she unworthy of love?

Is she stupid?

Or is she a Queen who was never taught or shown love by Daddy so she searched for him in the arms of those who weren't ready?

Or is she a Queen who had so much love to give but gave it to others and never gave it to herself?

Or is she a Queen who never believed she deserved more?

Or is she a Queen who had to get hurt enough times so when she met her King she could appreciate him?

Or is she a Queen who had to practice twice and warm up before the real game?

What is she? Who is she?

She is ME

# Be Patient with Me

Underneath my sarcastic responses to your
compliments is a small voice that has been dying to
say "Thank You".

I roll my eyes when you say you love me because the
little girl in me didn't hear it
enough.

I'm hard on you because I want to give you every
reason to leave and see if you will still stay.

Previous relationships have left me with a PTSD so
deep in my soul that it will take a real King to help me
heal.

I KNOW you are that King

You told me that you had visions of me before we
met but, for me, you are everything I thought I
couldn't have and everything I was told I didn't
deserve.

So be patient with me

As I allow those repressed tears to surface, spill over
and cleanse me.

Be patient with me

As I inhale your love and exhale the fucked up

definitions of love I have been taught to believe.

Be patient with me

As I learn to look in the mirror and see the purest form of me that you see.

Be patient with me

As I scrub off cold, unkind and even unwanted touches so I can fully absorb the warmth of your touch.

Be patient with me

As I detox mind body and spirit to completely take you in.

Be patient with me..........

# ABOUT THE AUTHOR

Tamykah Anthony-Marston is a 31 year old passionate and award winning scientist. Most people who know her know of her work and her commitment to inspire young people who look like her to pursue careers in the various fields of science. What most people do not know is what she has had to overcome to achieve her success. They do not know her story.

Before getting married on her 30th birthday (April 26th, 2015), she was a single mother of two children by two different men. In her relationships with the fathers of her two children, she has experienced physical abuse, verbal abuse, abandonment and so much more. Her journey from being a single teenage mother of one, to a single adult mother of two, to now a happily married woman expecting her third child has been filled with pain, sadness, anger and disappointment but has been nothing short of miraculous.

**Diary of a MisEducated Baby Mama** is an autobiographical poetic memoir of this journey.

Thank you for taking the time to read about my journey! I would love to hear from you!

For reviews, testimonials, responses and questions, please email:
miseducatedbabymama@gmail.com

Join the discussion at
www.miseducatedbabymama.wordpress.com